SCHOLASTIC

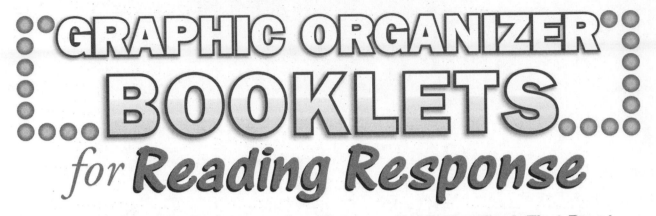

GRAPHIC ORGANIZER BOOKLETS
for *Reading Response*

Guided Response Packets for Any Fiction or Nonfiction Book That Boost Students' Comprehension—and Help You Manage Independent Reading

by Rhonda Graff Silver

NEW YORK • TORONTO • LONDON • AUCKLAND • SYDNEY
MEXICO CITY • NEW DELHI • HONG KONG • BUENOS AIRES

Teaching *Resources*

To Dr. Melvin Levine

Cover design by Jason Robinson
Interior design by Melinda Belter
Interior illustrations by Teresa Anderko

ISBN-13 978-0-439-66118-8
ISBN-10 0-439-66118-8

1 2 3 4 5 6 7 8 9 10   40   12 11 10 09 08 07

Table of Contents

Introduction

Using visual aids goes well beyond having students fill in worksheets. The graphic organizers in this book will help students learn necessary skills, actively participate in learning, and take part in discussions, all of which result in higher levels of thinking.

The Benefits of Using This Book

There are many benefits for teachers and students who use visual representations such as graphic organizers, webs, and maps.

- Organizers help students focus on key points instead of overwhelming them with pages of information.

- Organizers encourage students to make connections, identify relationships, and see information in new ways.

- When organizers are used, students think and write about what they read. They have the opportunity to share what they've read as they discuss their responses on the organizers.

How to Use This Book

This book is arranged into eight six-page student booklets. Each booklet focuses on either a genre or a theme related to nonfiction or fiction. The booklets can be reproduced back-to-back and then stapled together to form a spine.

A teacher page accompanies each booklet. This page includes the following:

❧ a reduced page with sample answers using exemplary text(s)

❧ instructional points, discussion starters, and/or teacher tips

Each student booklet contains a cover page, related activity pages, and a personal response page.

❧ The cover page includes space for students to fill in information about the book or resource being used and a space for them to record their prior knowledge or related personal experience.

❧ The middle pages consist of related organizers, charts, and webs.

❧ The last page of each booklet is a personal response page, which allows students to integrate the knowledge they obtained from the study with personal ideas, thoughts, questions and discussion prompts. (NOTE: It's important for students to provide personal responses, but be sure they are using the new information related to their study and not overusing unrelated personal judgments.)

Background Information

Although detailed directions appear on each page of a booklet, students will still need direct and explicit instruction in order to learn how to complete these graphic organizer activities successfully and meaningfully. Sharing a completed organizer and modeling the process of completion will benefit students and move them toward independence. It is important not only to model "how to" but also to model the thinking process that occurs as an activity is completed. As with all skills, practice and feedback are crucial to achieving automaticity.

 It is not necessary to require an in-depth response for every book that students read. However, when students choose a book to use with a booklet, they should understand that the focus is not on completing every question on every page but rather on the importance of discussing, questioning, and learning from peers. The goal is to achieve a higher level of thinking and understanding. Always encourage students to elaborate on and explain their responses. Use the organizers to help them plan, organize, and share information about what they've read and learned. Note students' different strengths and how they are able to share what they really know. The feedback and interaction will help promote true learning and growth.

Students should discuss how the organizers worked for them, noting possible changes to the organizers they present. Their creativity may offer new insights and alternative ways of meeting the goals. Students should be encouraged to create their own graphic organizers to assist in their learning. If these activities are to foster higher-level thinking, then students must be guided in that direction.

The literacy organizers in this book support the following standards outlined by the New York State Education Department Virtual Learning System and the Mid-continental Regional Educational Laboratory (McREL). (Other state and regional standards can certainly be supported as well; however, due to the variety of standards across different geographical areas, it's not easy to compile a comprehensive list of standards.) As they work with the organizers, students will do the following:

❧ read, write, listen, and speak for information and understanding

❧ read, write, listen, and speak for literacy expression

❧ read, write, listen, and speak for critical analysis and evaluation

❧ read, write, listen, and speak for social interaction

❧ gather and use information for research purposes

❧ use the general skills and strategies of the reading process

❧ use reading skills and strategies to understand and interpret a variety of literary texts

❧ use reading skills and strategies to understand and interpret a variety of informational texts

❧ use listening and speaking strategies for different purposes

When students read with a goal in mind, they will be more likely to focus on what they are reading. The purpose of using these graphic organizer booklets is to have students internalize these skills so that they will be better able to organize their own thoughts, ideas, and questions. With experience, students can begin to produce their own graphic organizers.

The optimal outcome is to create strong, critical readers who truly enjoy reading and learning. With this framework, students can better understand what they read throughout their school years and into adulthood.

Helpful Hints for the Biography Booklet:

- Model each activity as often as necessary to ensure that students understand its purpose as well as the directions.

- Remind students to preview the pages of the booklet so they are aware of pre-reading, during-reading, and post-reading activities.

- Show students how to use the text to support an answer. A response is stronger when it is supported by proof. Students will need to reread and think about what they've read. As they read, they may want to "mark" the text to help them remember key points of interest, quotes, or key events.

Exemplary texts:

You Want Women to Vote, Lizzie Stanton? by Jean Fritz (G. P. Putnam's Sons, 1995)

Rabble Rousers by Cheryl Harness (Dutton Children's Books, 2003)

The Road to Seneca Falls by Gwenyth Swain (Carolrhoda Books, 1996)

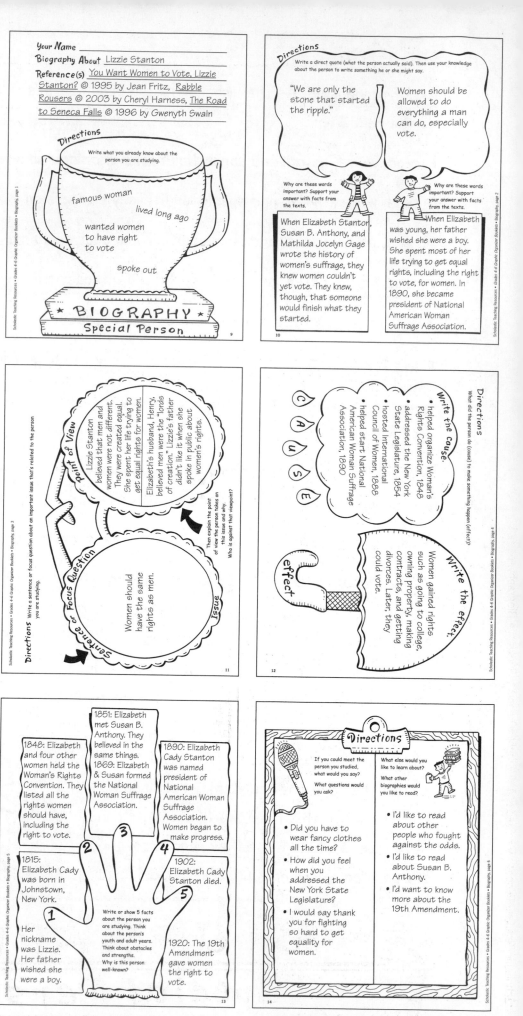

Your Name _____

Biography About _____

Reference(s) _____

_____

_____

_____

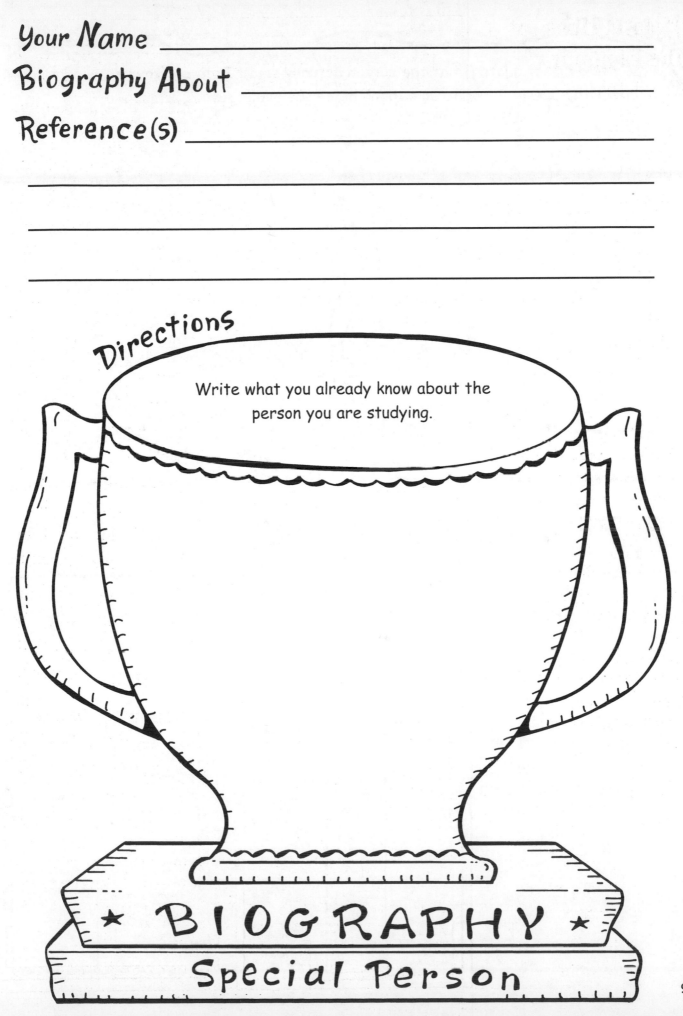

Directions

Write what you already know about the person you are studying.

★ B I O G R A P H Y ★

Special Person

Directions

Write a direct quote (what the person actually said). Then use your knowledge about the person to write something he or she might say.

Why are these words important? Support your answer with facts from the texts.

Why are these words important? Support your answer with facts from the texts.

Scholastic Teaching Resources • Grades 4–6 Graphic Organizer Booklets • Biography, page 2

Directions Write a sentence or focus question about an important issue that's related to the person you are studying.

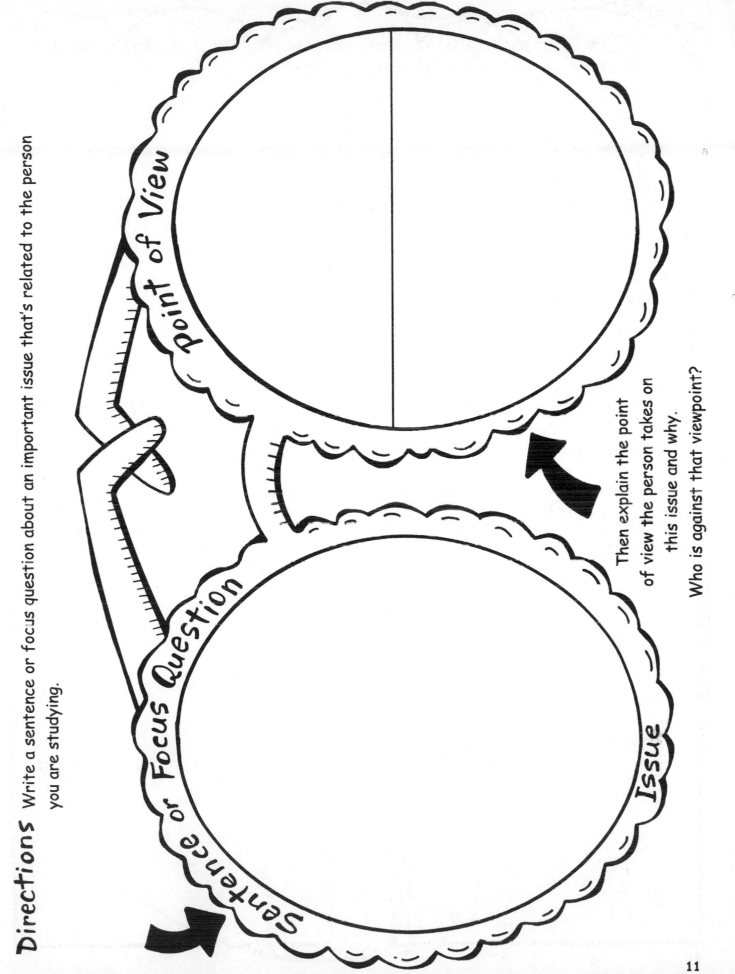

Point of View

Sentence or Focus Question

Issue

Then explain the point of view the person takes on this issue and why. Who is against that viewpoint?

Directions

What did the person do (cause) to make something happen (effect)?

Write the cause.

C A u S E

Write the effect.

effect

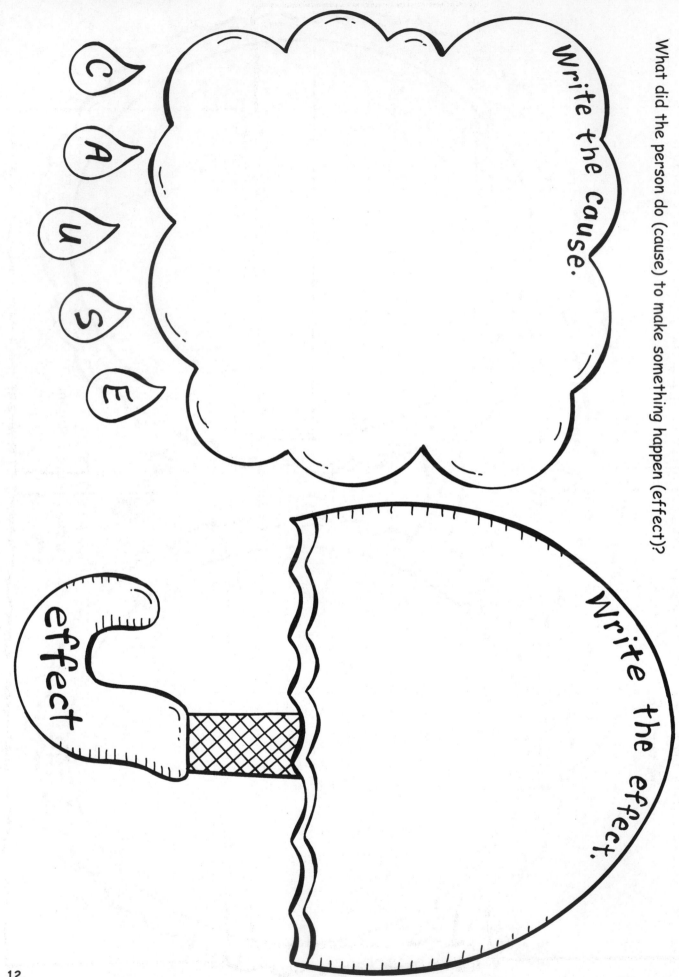

Scholastic Teaching Resources • Grades 4–6 Graphic Organizer Booklets • Biography, page 4

1

2

3

4

5

Write or show 5 facts about the person you are studying. Think about the person's youth and adult years. Think about obstacles and strengths. Why is this person well-known?

If you could meet the person you studied, what would you say?

What questions would you ask?

What else would you like to learn about?

What other biographies would you like to read?

Scholastic Teaching Resources • Grades 4–6 Graphic Organizer Booklets • Biography, page 6

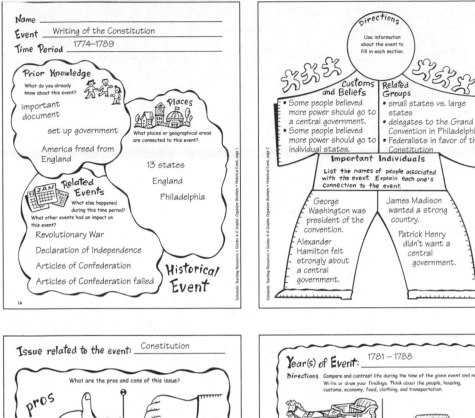

Page 16

Name _____

Event Writing of the Constitution

Time Period 1774–1789

Prior Knowledge
What do you already know about this event?

important document

set up government

America freed from England

Places
What places or geographical areas are connected to this event?

13 states

England

Philadelphia

Related Events
What else happened during this time period? What other events had an impact on this event?

Revolutionary War

Declaration of Independence

Articles of Confederation

Articles of Confederation failed

Historical Event

16

Scholastic Teaching Resources • Grades 4–6 Graphic Organizer Booklets • Historical Event, page 1

Page 17

Directions
Use information about the event to fill in each section.

Customs and Beliefs
• Some people believed more power should go to a central government.
• Some people believed more power should go to individual states.

Related Groups
• small states vs. large states
• delegates to the Grand Convention in Philadelphia
• Federalists in favor of the Constitution

Important Individuals
List the names of people associated with the event. Explain each one's connection to the event.

George Washington was president of the convention.

Alexander Hamilton felt strongly about a central government.

James Madison wanted a strong country.

Patrick Henry didn't want a central government.

17

Scholastic Teaching Resources • Grades 4–6 Graphic Organizer Booklets • Historical Event, page 2

Page 18

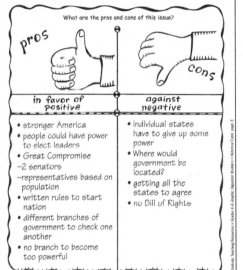

Issue related to the event: ___Constitution___

What are the pros and cons of this issue?

pros

cons

in favor of positive	against negative
• stronger America	• individual states have to give up some power
• people could have power to elect leaders	• Where would government be located?
• Great Compromise	• getting all the states to agree
–2 senators	• no Bill of Rights
–representatives based on population	
• written rules to start nation	
• different branches of government to check one another	
• no branch to become too powerful	

18

Scholastic Teaching Resources • Grades 4–6 Graphic Organizer Booklets • Historical Event, page 3

Page 19

Year(s) of Event: 1781 – 1788

Directions Compare and contrast life during the time of the given event and now. Write or draw your findings. Think about the people, housing, customs, economy, food, clothing, and transportation.

Then	Now
There was slavery in the South.	There is no more slavery in the U.S.
Women had little to do outside the home.	Women have more freedom and choices.
Children played with toys like balls, marbles, dolls.	Children still play with balls, marbles, and dolls, but they also play with electronic toys and video games.

19

Scholastic Teaching Resources • Grades 4–6 Graphic Organizer Booklets • Historical Event, page 4

Page 20

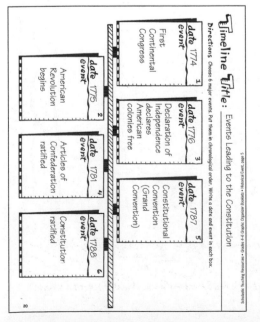

Timeline Title: _____ Events Leading to the Constitution

Directions Choose 6 major events. Put them in chronological order. Write a date and event in each box.

1. event date 1774 First Continental Congress
2. event date 1775 American Revolution begins
3. event date 1776 Declaration of Independence declares American colonies free
4. event date 1781 Articles of Confederation ratified
5. event date 1787 Constitutional Convention (Grand Convention)
6. event date 1788 Constitution ratified

20

Scholastic Teaching Resources • Grades 4–6 Graphic Organizer Booklets • Historical Event, page 5

Page 21

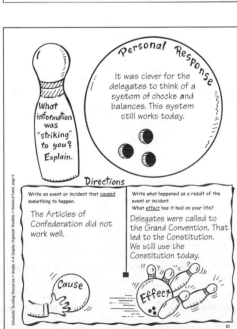

Personal Response

It was clever for the delegates to think of a system of checks and balances. This system still works today.

What information was "striking" to you? Explain.

Directions

Write an event or incident that *caused* something to happen.

The Articles of Confederation did not work well.

Write what happened as a result of the event or incident. What *effect* has it had on your life?

Delegates were called to the Grand Convention. That led to the Constitution. We still use the Constitution today.

Cause

Effect

21

Scholastic Teaching Resources • Grades 4–6 Graphic Organizer Booklets • Historical Event, page 6

Helpful Hints for the Historical Event Booklet:

• Model each activity for students to make sure they understand its purpose as well as the directions. Repeat the modeling if necessary.

• Remind students to preview the pages of the booklet so they are aware of pre-reading, during-reading, and post-reading activities.

• Welcome student input and feedback. Think of these booklets as starting points. The goal is to have students better understand what they read. As they develop the necessary foundation, they will begin to create their own ways of understanding and will have a better sense of the written words around them. Over time, we hope this becomes automatic.

Exemplary texts:

Shh! We're Writing the Constitution by Jean Fritz (G. P. Putnam's Sons, 1987)

...If You Were There When They Signed the Constitution by Elizabeth Levy (Scholastic, 1987)

Name _____

Event _____

Time Period _____

Prior Knowledge

What do you already know about this event?

Places

What places or geographical areas are connected to this event?

Related Events

What else happened during this time period?

What other events had an impact on this event?

Historical Event

Scholastic Teaching Resources • Grades 4–6 Graphic Organizer Booklets • Historical Event, page 1

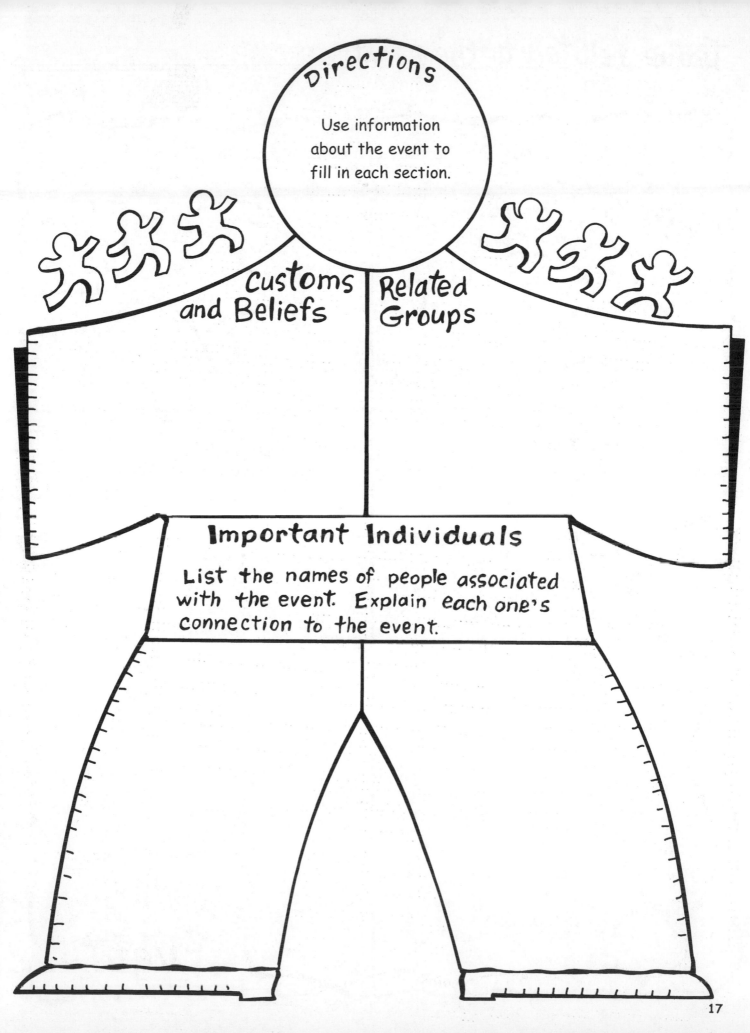

Directions

Use information
about the event to
fill in each section.

Customs
and Beliefs

Related
Groups

Important Individuals

List the names of people associated
with the event. Explain each one's
connection to the event.

Issue related to the event: _____

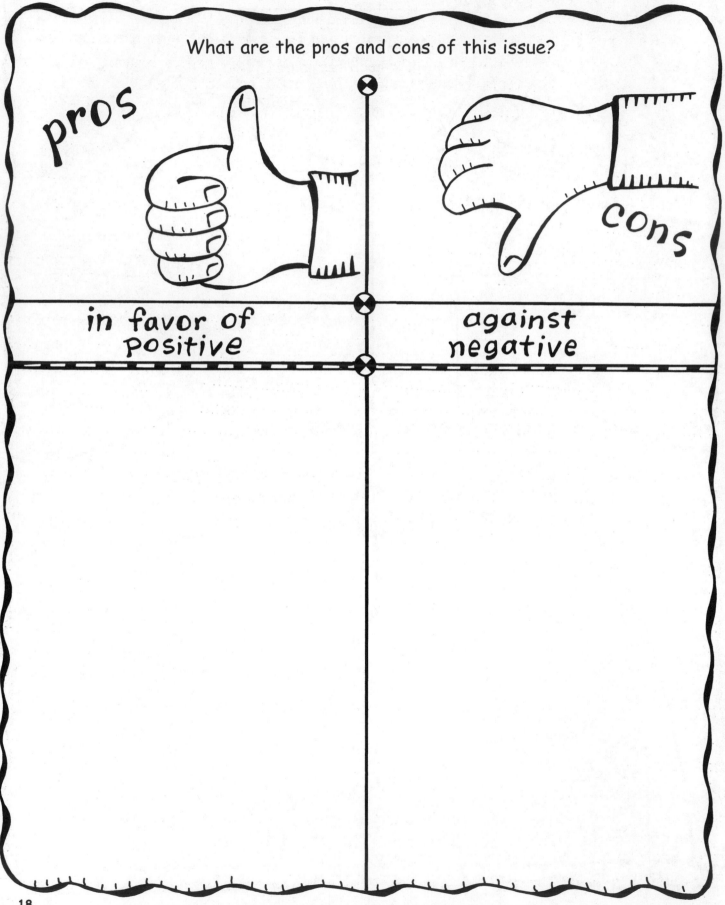

What are the pros and cons of this issue?

pros

cons

in favor of
positive

against
negative

Scholastic Teaching Resources • Grades 4–6 Graphic Organizer Booklets • Historical Event, page 3

Year(s) of Event: _____

Directions Compare and contrast life during the time of the given event and now. Write or draw your findings. Think about the people, housing, customs, economy, food, clothing, and transportation.

Then	Now

Timeline Title: _____

Directions Choose 6 major events. Put them in chronological order. Write a date and event in each box.

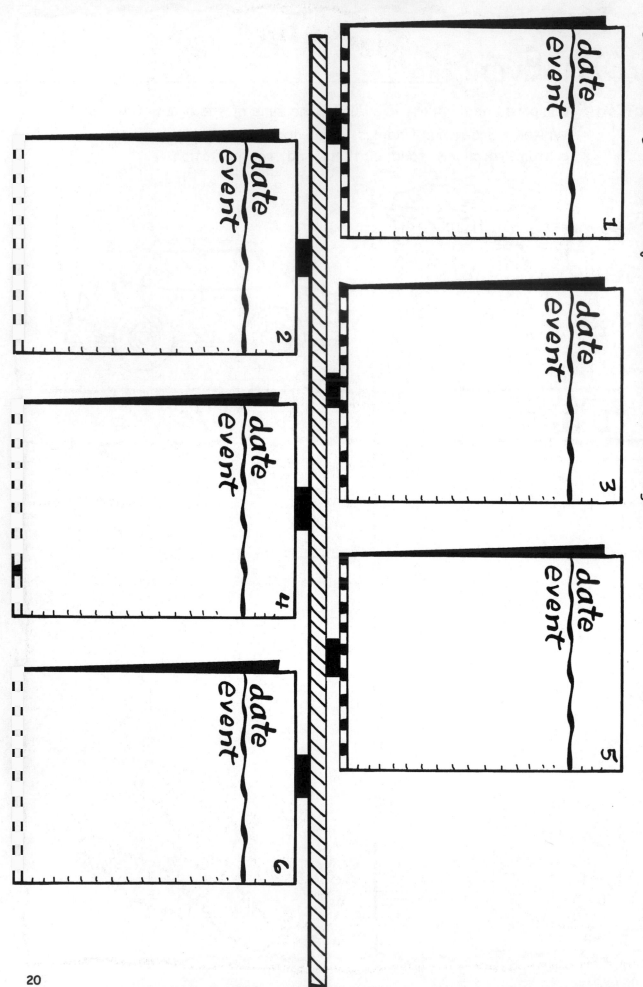

date
event

1

date
event

3

date
event

5

date
event

2

date
event

4

date
event

6

Scholastic Teaching Resources • Grades 4–6 Graphic Organizer Booklets • Historical Event, page 5

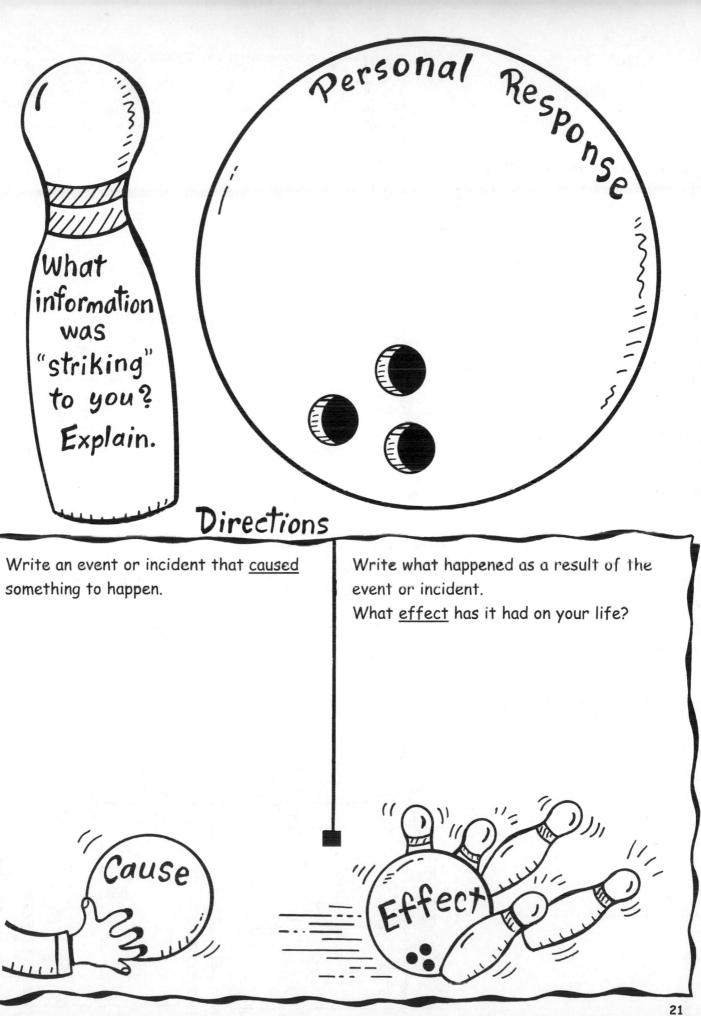

Personal Response

What information was "striking" to you? Explain.

Directions

Write an event or incident that <u>caused</u> something to happen.

Write what happened as a result of the event or incident.
What <u>effect</u> has it had on your life?

Cause

Effect

Scholastic Teaching Resources • Grades 4–6 Graphic Organizer Booklets • Historical Event, page 6

Helpful Hints for the Geographical Location Booklet:

- Model each activity for students as often as necessary to ensure that they understand its purpose as well as the directions.

- Remind students to preview the pages of the booklet so they are aware of pre-reading, during-reading, and post-reading activities.

- In this booklet, students are given the opportunity to draw. Some students will use these picture supports as a way to help them express themselves verbally. This will help them gain confidence and skill to move to written expression. (Be aware of different learning styles and outcomes. Some students will always respond better through illustration.)

Exemplary texts:

Taking Your Camera to Mexico by Ted Park (Steck-Vaughn, 2000)

Dropping In on. . .Mexico by Lewis K. Parker (Rourke Publishing, 1994)

Mexico: Giant of the South by Eileen Latell Smith (Dillon Press, 1983)

Mexico (Enchantment of the World) by R. Conrad Stein (Children's Press, 1994)

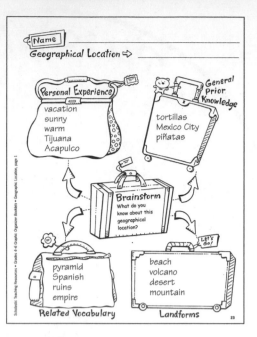

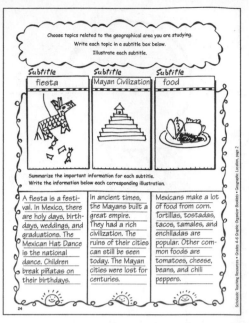

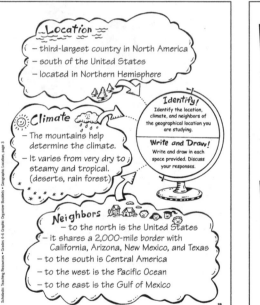

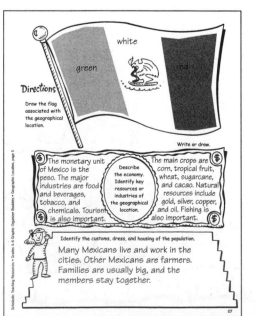

Name _____

Geographical Location ⇨ _____

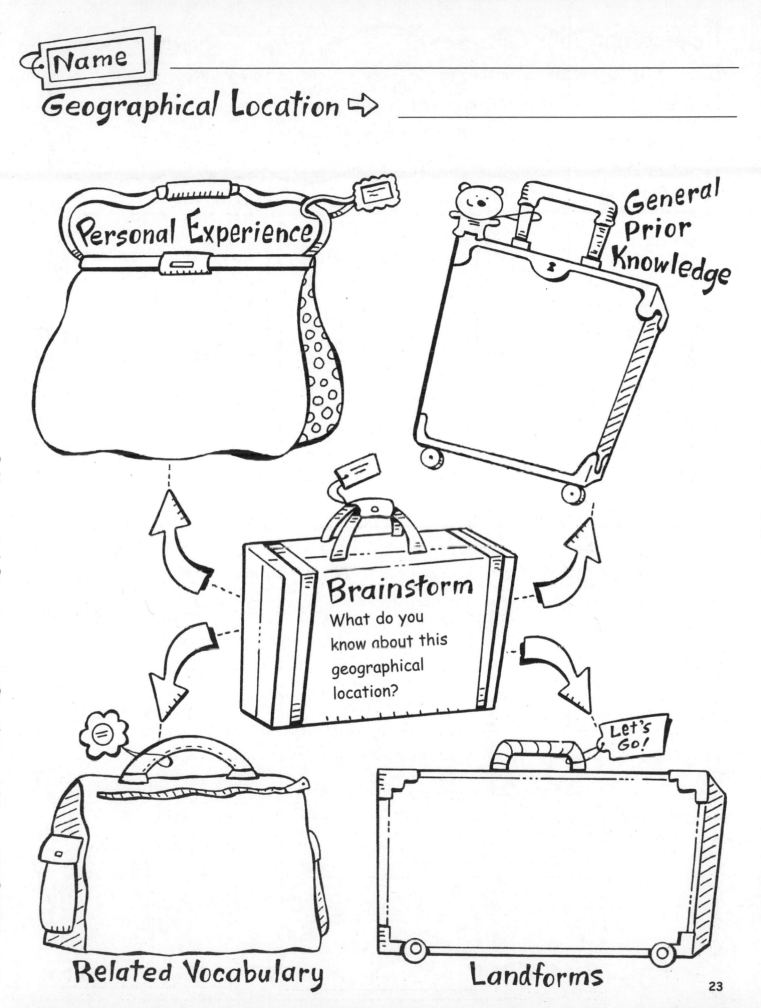

Personal Experience

General Prior Knowledge

Brainstorm
What do you know about this geographical location?

Let's Go!

Related Vocabulary

Landforms

Choose topics related to the geographical area you are studying.

Write each topic in a subtitle box below.

Illustrate each subtitle.

Subtitle   Subtitle   Subtitle

Summarize the important information for each subtitle.

Write the information below each corresponding illustration.

Scholastic Teaching Resources • Grades 4–6 Graphic Organizer Booklets • Geographical Location, page 2

Location

Climate

Identify!
Identify the location, climate, and neighbors of the geographical location you are studying.

Write and Draw!
Write and draw in each space provided. Discuss your responses.

Neighbors

In the large boxes, draw special places and landmarks located in your geographical location. Label them.

In the set of three adjoining boxes, describe these places and landmarks. Explain why they are important.

Scholastic Teaching Resources • Grades 4–6 Graphic Organizer Booklets • Geographical Location, page 4

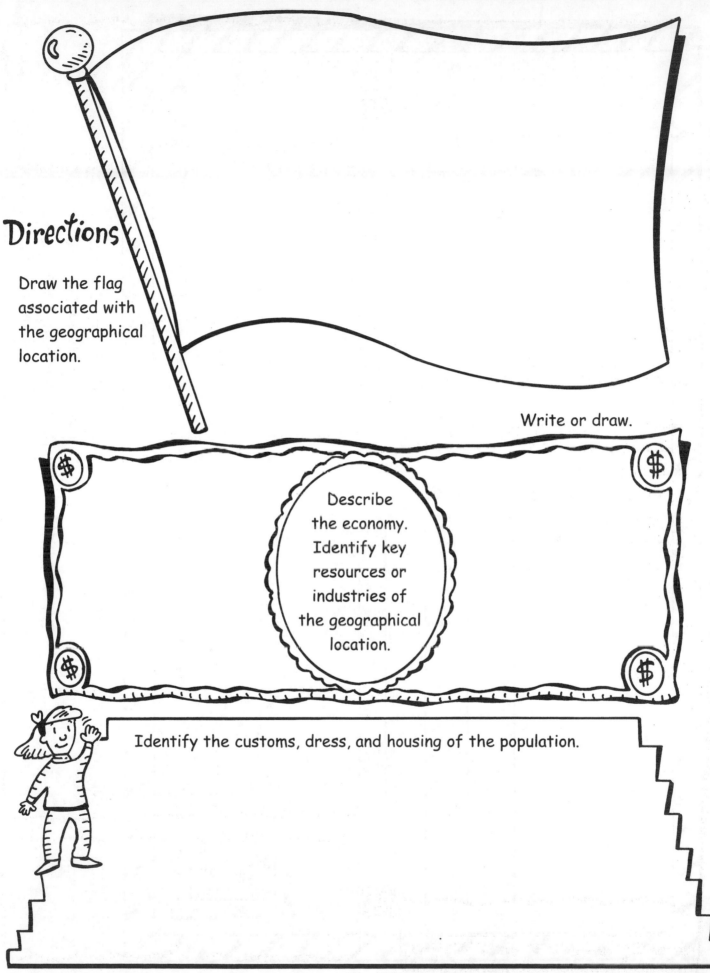

Directions

Draw the flag associated with the geographical location.

Write or draw.

Describe the economy. Identify key resources or industries of the geographical location.

Identify the customs, dress, and housing of the population.

Directions

Write a postcard to a friend or someone in your family.

Tell about the geographical location you are studying.

Include at least three important facts.

Think about the people, culture, economy, interesting sights, and weather.

Correspondence

July 10

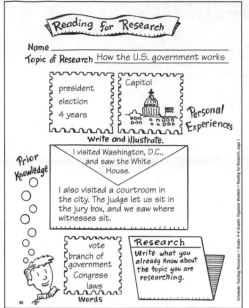

Reading for Research

Name _____
Topic of Research How the U.S. government works

president
election
4 years

Capitol

Personal Experiences

Write and Illustrate

Prior Knowledge

I visited Washington, D.C., and saw the White House.

I also visited a courtroom in the city. The judge let us sit in the jury box, and we saw where witnesses sit.

vote
branch of government
Congress
laws

Research
Write what you already know about the topic you are researching.

Words

30

Fishing for Facts

judicial branch | The U.S. Supreme Court. | • Disagreements that go to court are called cases. • All courts are part of the judicial branch. • Supreme Court is the highest court. • 9 justices on Supreme Court

legislative branch | The U.S. Congress | • each state represented • U.S. Senate (2 from each state, 6-year term) • House of Representatives (based upon population, 2-year term) • branch that makes laws

executive branch | Our Presidency 7-13 | • President • Chief Executive • represents all Americans • Commander-in-Chief • can make treaties, appoint ambassadors, set foreign policy • can suggest bills to Congress

Directions
Fill in specific topics you want to research.

Document your source of information. Include any page numbers.

Record information as you read. Include these:
- facts
- notes
- questions
- illustrations

31

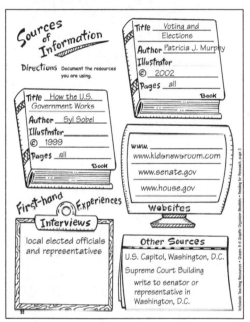

Sources of Information

Directions Document the resources you are using.

Title How the U.S. Government Works
Author Syl Sobel
Illustrator
© 1999
Pages all
Book

Title Voting and Elections
Author Patricia J. Murphy
Illustrator
© 2002
Pages all
Book

www.kidsnewsroom.com
www.senate.gov
www.house.gov
Websites

First-hand Experiences
Interviews
local elected officials and representatives

Other Sources
U.S. Capitol, Washington, D.C.
Supreme Court Building
write to senator or representative in Washington, D.C.

32

Outline It

Focus Idea U.S. Government _____

I. Three branches of government
   A. the legislative branch
   B. the executive branch
   C. the judicial branch

II. The president
   A. elected every four years
   B. in charge of the military
   C. works with leaders from other countries

III. People of the United States
   A. vote
   B. pay taxes
   C. some serve in the armed forces

33

Directions
Use information from your research to write questions and to document something you found intriguing or exciting.

As you read, answer your question with information or new questions. Use all your sources. Write and illustrate.

? | Why do people pay taxes? | Taxes help the government pay for highways, bridges, military supplies, and government workers.
Source: How the U.S. Government Works

? | Why do we need the Supreme Court? | The Supreme Court decides what the Constitution means and decides if a law is unconstitutional.
Source: Our Supreme Court

? | What is a political party? | A political party is a group of people who share the same ideas. In the U.S., the two main political parties are the Democrats and the Republicans.
Source: Voting and Elections

! | A president can be elected even if he or she does not win the popular vote. | The popular vote doesn't elect the president. Each state sends electors to Electoral College. Each state's electors equal the number of its senators and representatives.
Source: Our Presidency

34

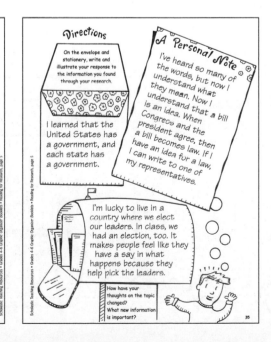

Directions
On the envelope and stationery, write and illustrate your response to the information you found through your research.

I learned that the United States has a government, and each state has a government.

A Personal Note
I've heard so many of the words, but now I understand what they mean. Now I understand that a bill is an idea. When Congress and the president agree, then a bill becomes law. If I have an idea for a law, I can write to one of my representatives.

I'm lucky to live in a country where we elect our leaders. In class, we had an election, too. It makes people feel like they have a say in what happens because they help pick the leaders.

How have your thoughts on the topic changed? What new information is important?

35

Helpful Hints for the Reading for Research Booklet:

- Model each activity for students as often as necessary to ensure that they understand its purpose as well as the directions.

- Remind students to preview the pages of the booklet so they are aware of pre-reading, during-reading, and post-reading activities.

- Familiarize students with the layout of nonfiction books, including their textbooks. Point out the use of photos, captions, maps, graphs, diagrams, heads and subheads, and differences in typeface. Emphasize the importance of knowing how to interpret information presented in a variety of forms.

- On page 5, students are asked to formulate questions. Writing *why* and *how* questions requires students to think at a higher level than when they write *who*, *what*, *where*, and *when* questions, which can usually be answered more directly.

Exemplary texts:

Our Supreme Court by Meish Goldish (The Millbrook Press, 1994)

The U.S. Congress by Patricia J. Murphy (Compass Point Books, 2002)

Voting and Elections by Patricia J. Murphy (Compass Point Books, 2002)

How the U.S. Government Works by Syl Sobel (Barron's 1999)

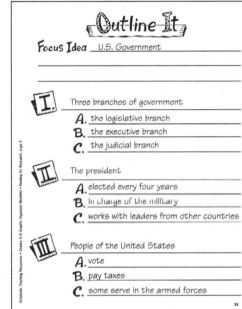

Reading for Research

Name _____

Topic of Research _____

Personal Experiences

Write and illustrate.

Prior Knowledge

Words

Research

Write what you already know about the topic you are researching.

Scholastic Teaching Resources • Grades 4–6 Graphic Organizer Booklets • Reading for Research, page 1

Fishing for Facts

Directions

Fill in specific topics you want to research.

Document your source of information. Include any page numbers.

Record information as you read. Include these:

- facts
- notes
- questions
- illustrations

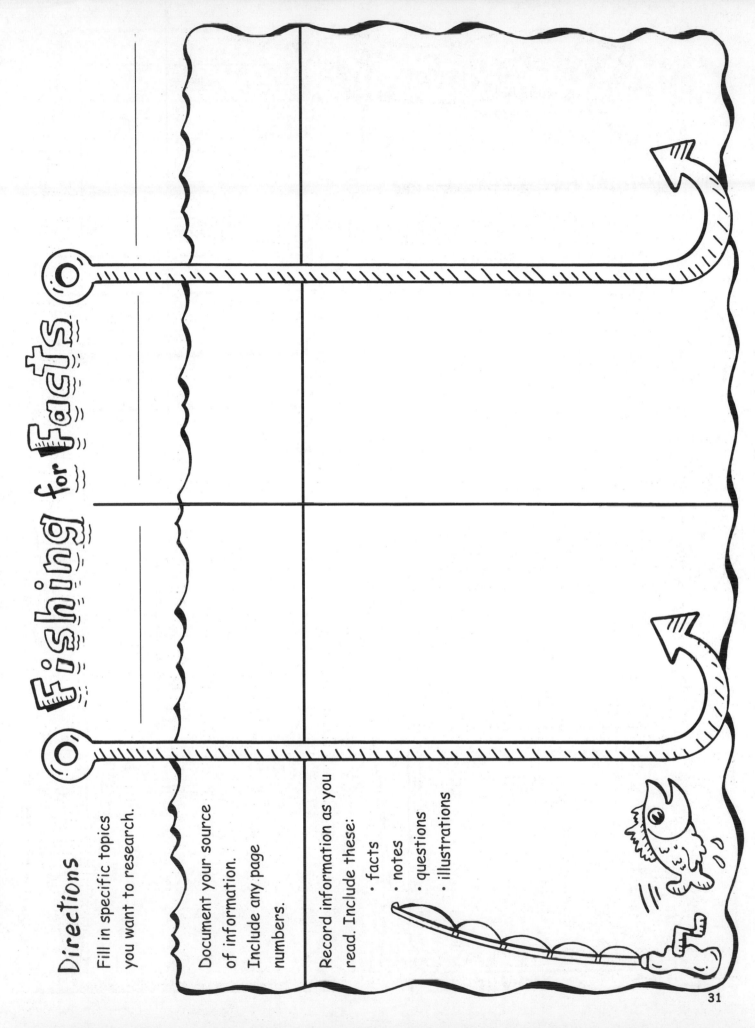

Sources of Information

Directions Document the resources you are using.

Book (top right)

Title _____

_____

Author _____

Illustrator _____

© _____

Pages _____

Book

Book (left)

Title _____

_____

Author _____

Illustrator _____

© _____

Pages _____

Book

Websites

www. _____

_____

_____

_____

Websites

First-hand Experiences

Interviews

Other Sources

Scholastic Teaching Resources • Grades 4–6 Graphic Organizer Booklets • Reading for Research, page 3

Outline It

Focus Idea _____

_____

_____

I. _____

    A. _____

    B. _____

    C. _____

II. _____

    A. _____

    B. _____

    C. _____

III. _____

    A. _____

    B. _____

    C. _____

Directions

Use information from your research to write questions and to document something you found intriguing or exciting.

As you read, answer your question with information or new questions. Use all your sources. Write and illustrate.

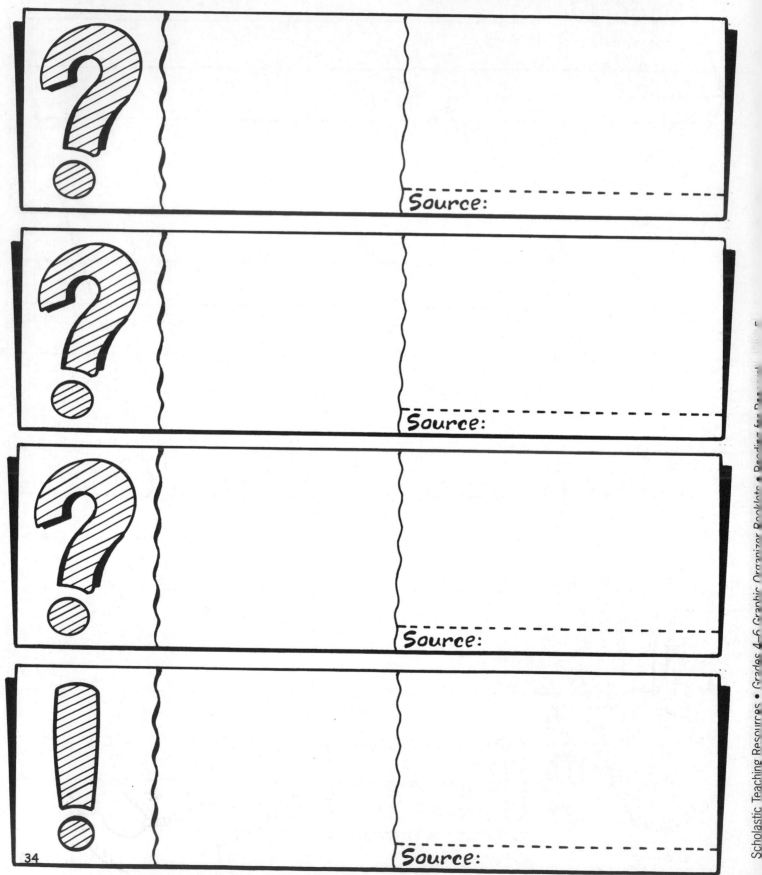

Source:

Source:

Source:

Source:

34

Directions

On the envelope and stationery, write and illustrate your response to the information you found through your research.

A Personal Note

How have your thoughts on the topic changed?
What new information is important?

Helpful Hints for the Nonfiction Booklet:

- Model each activity as often as necessary so students understand its purpose as well as the directions.

- Remind students to preview the pages of the booklet so they are aware of pre-reading, during-reading, and post-reading activities.

- You may choose to write vocabulary words before copying page 5. By doing this, you can focus students' attention on specific words and make the activity more directed. This can also help you provide differentiated instruction for those students who may need more support.

- When students are asked to make a prediction or formulate questions, be sure they consider how their thoughts, responses, and questions changed as they read. These activities can lead to worthwhile discussions.

Exemplary text:

Cornerstones of Freedom: Ellis Island by R. Conrad Stein (Children's Press, 1992)

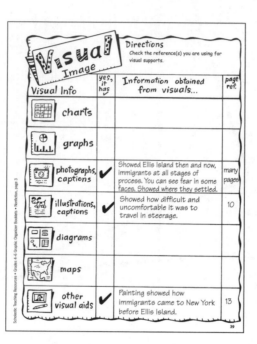

Name _____
Topic _Ellis Island/immigration_
Book or Article _Cornerstones of Freedom: Ellis Island_
Author/Illustrator _R. Conrad Stein_
Copyright© _1992_

★ Write ★ Draw ★ Question ★ Predict ★

Europe   hope

freedom   England

New World   New York City

immigration

What do you know about your topic already?

Nonfiction

Questions & Answers

Before or while you read, write questions for each box below. (Some boxes may be left blank.)

As you read and learn, write and draw responses to your questions.

	Questions	Answers
Who?	Who came to America?	People from Russia, Poland, Yugoslavia, southern Germany, Italy, Greece, England, and Ireland came to America.
What?	What is Ellis Island?	It was an immigration center in New York. Immigrants stopped there to see if they could stay in the United States.
Where?	Where did the immigrants go when they came to the United States?	First they went to the Registry Room to be examined by doctors and questioned by officers.
When?	When have people come to the United States?	1600–1776 (Colonial) 1776–1890 (old immigration) 1890–early 1900s (new immigration)
Why?	Why did people come to the United States?	They had hope for better lives.
How?	How long did it take to cross the Atlantic Ocean?	It took about 3 weeks by boat.

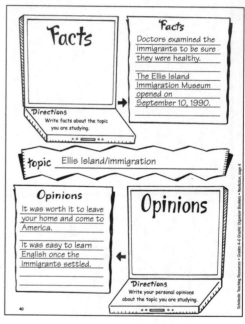

Visual Image

Directions: Check the reference(s) you are using for visual supports.

Visual Info	yes, it has	Information obtained from visuals...	page ref.
charts			
graphs			
photographs, captions	✔	Showed Ellis Island then and now, immigrants at all stages of process. You can see fear in some faces. Showed where they settled.	many pages
illustrations, captions	✔	Showed how difficult and uncomfortable it was to travel in steerage.	10
diagrams			
maps			
other visual aids	✔	Painting showed how immigrants came to New York before Ellis Island.	13

Facts

Directions: Write facts about the topic you are studying.

Doctors examined the immigrants to be sure they were healthy.

The Ellis Island Immigration Museum opened on September 10, 1990.

topic _Ellis Island/immigration_

Opinions

Directions: Write your personal opinions about the topic you are studying.

It was worth it to leave your home and come to America.

It was easy to learn English once the immigrants settled.

BEFORE READING
List any words you already know that are related to the topic.

immigrant

Vocabulary

AFTER READING Choose two new vocabulary words from the text.

Write one new word in the box.

steerage

It means... usually the lowest deck of a ship

Use the word in a sentence. It was dark and dirty in steerage so many passengers were uncomfortable.

Write the other new word in the box.

interpreter

It means... someone who explains or translates

Use the word in a sentence. The man spoke Russian so he needed an interpreter to understand the rules.

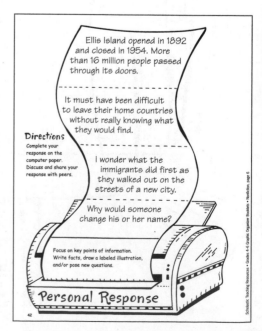

Ellis Island opened in 1892 and closed in 1954. More than 16 million people passed through its doors.

It must have been difficult to leave their home countries without really knowing what they would find.

Directions: Complete your response on the computer paper. Discuss and share your response with peers.

I wonder what the immigrants did first as they walked out on the streets of a new city.

Why would someone change his or her name?

Focus on key points of information. Write facts, draw a labeled illustration, and/or pose new questions.

Personal Response

Name _____

Topic _____

Book or Article _____

Author/Illustrator _____

Copyright© _____

★ Write ★ Draw ★ Question ★ Predict ★

What do you know about your topic already?

Nonfiction

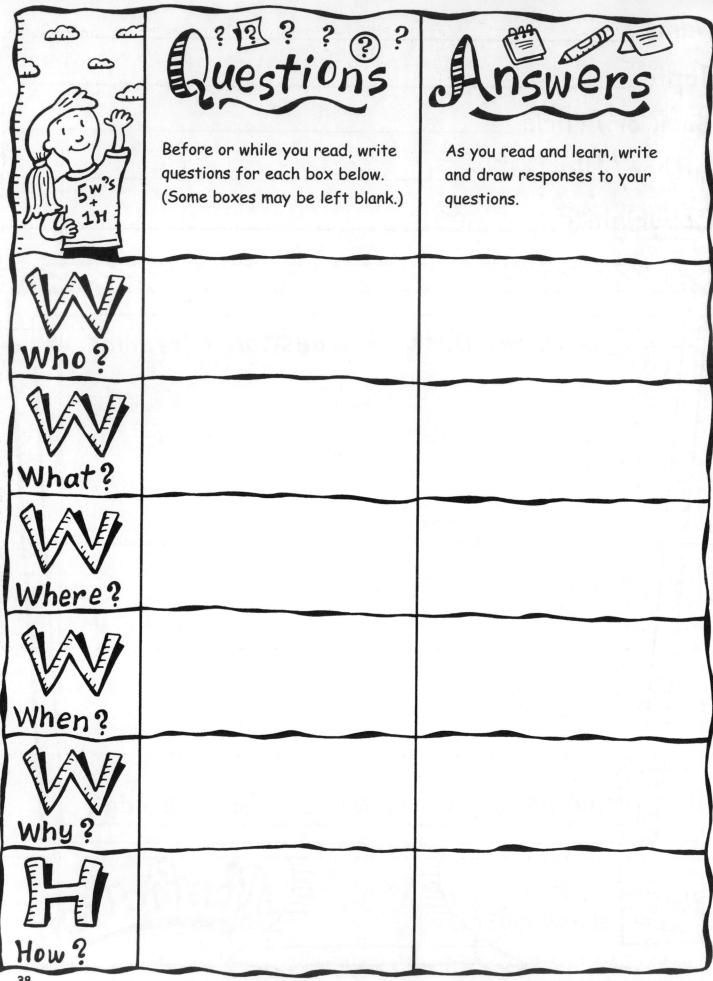

Questions

Before or while you read, write questions for each box below. (Some boxes may be left blank.)

Answers

As you read and learn, write and draw responses to your questions.

5 w's + 1 H

W Who?

W What?

W Where?

W When?

W Why?

H How?

38

Visual Image

Check the reference(s) you are using for visual supports.

Visual Info	yes, it has ✓	Information obtained from visuals...	page ref.
charts			
graphs			
photographs, captions			
illustrations, captions			
diagrams			
maps			
other visual aids			

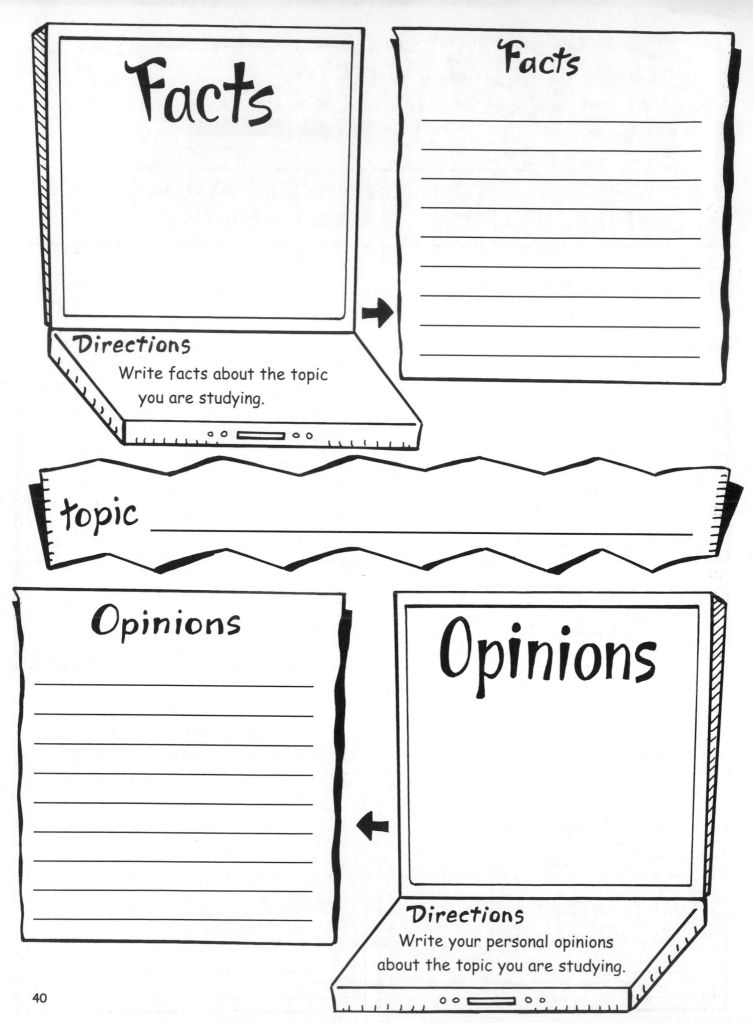

Facts

Facts

_____
_____
_____
_____
_____
_____
_____
_____

Directions

Write facts about the topic you are studying.

topic _____

Opinions

_____
_____
_____
_____
_____
_____
_____
_____

Opinions

Directions

Write your personal opinions about the topic you are studying.

40

BEFORE READING
List any words you already know that are related to the topic.

Vocabulary

AFTER READING Choose two new vocabulary words from the text.

Write one new word in the box.

It means...

Use the word in a sentence.

Write the other new word in the box.

It means...

Use the word in a sentence.

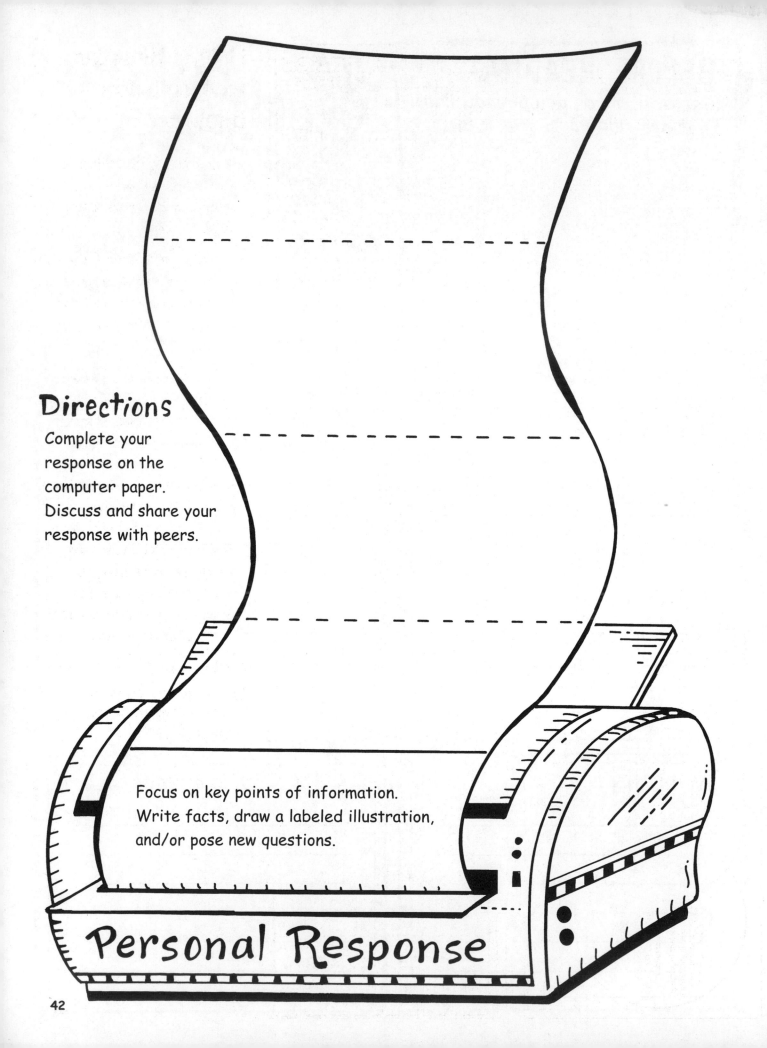

Directions

Complete your response on the computer paper. Discuss and share your response with peers.

Focus on key points of information. Write facts, draw a labeled illustration, and/or pose new questions.

Personal Response

Scholastic Teaching Resources • Grades 4–6 Graphic Organizer Booklets • Nonfiction, page 6

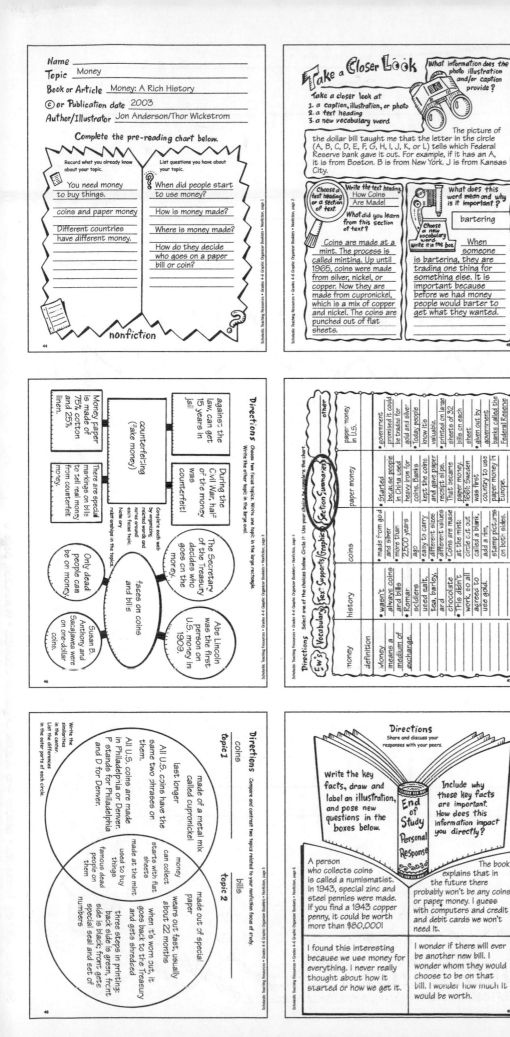

Helpful Hints for the Nonfiction Booklet:

- Model each activity as often as necessary so students understand its purpose as well as the directions.

- Remind students to preview the pages of the booklet so they are aware of pre-reading, during-reading, and post-reading activities.

- On page 6, students are asked to share their responses with peers. It is critical that students talk about how they arrived at their responses. It's also important for them to hear other points of view. With these discussions, students will have a deeper understanding and will see alternative viewpoints. Be sure to model and guide these discussions so students can see how to benefit from them.

Exemplary text:

Money: A Rich History by Jon Anderson (Grosset & Dunlap, 2003)

Name _____

Topic _____

Book or Article _____

© or Publication date _____

Author/Illustrator _____

Complete the pre-reading chart below.

Record what you already know about your topic.

List questions you have about your topic.

_____

• _____

_____

_____

_____

_____

_____

_____

_____

_____

_____

_____

_____

_____

_____

_____

_____

_____

nonfiction

Take a Closer Look

What information does the photo illustration and/or caption provide?

Take a closer look at
1. a caption, illustration, or photo
2. a text heading
3. a new vocabulary word

Choose a text heading or a section of text.

Write the text heading.

_____

_____

What did you learn from this section of text?

_____

_____

_____

_____

_____

_____

_____

_____

_____

What does this word mean and why is it important?

Choose a new vocabulary word. Write it in the box.

_____

_____

_____

_____

_____

_____

_____

_____

_____

_____

Directions

Choose two focus topics. Write one topic in the large rectangle.
Write the other topic in the large oval.

Complete each web by organizing related words and notes around each focus topic.

Note any relationships in the topics.

Scholastic Teaching Resources • Grades 4–6 Graphic Organizer Booklets • Nonfiction, page 3

Scholastic Teaching Resources • Grades 4–6 Graphic Organizer Booklets • Nonfiction, page 4

Directions Select one of the choices below. Circle it. Use your choice to complete the chart.

5w's   Vocabulary   Text Supports/Graphics   Section Summaries   _____ other

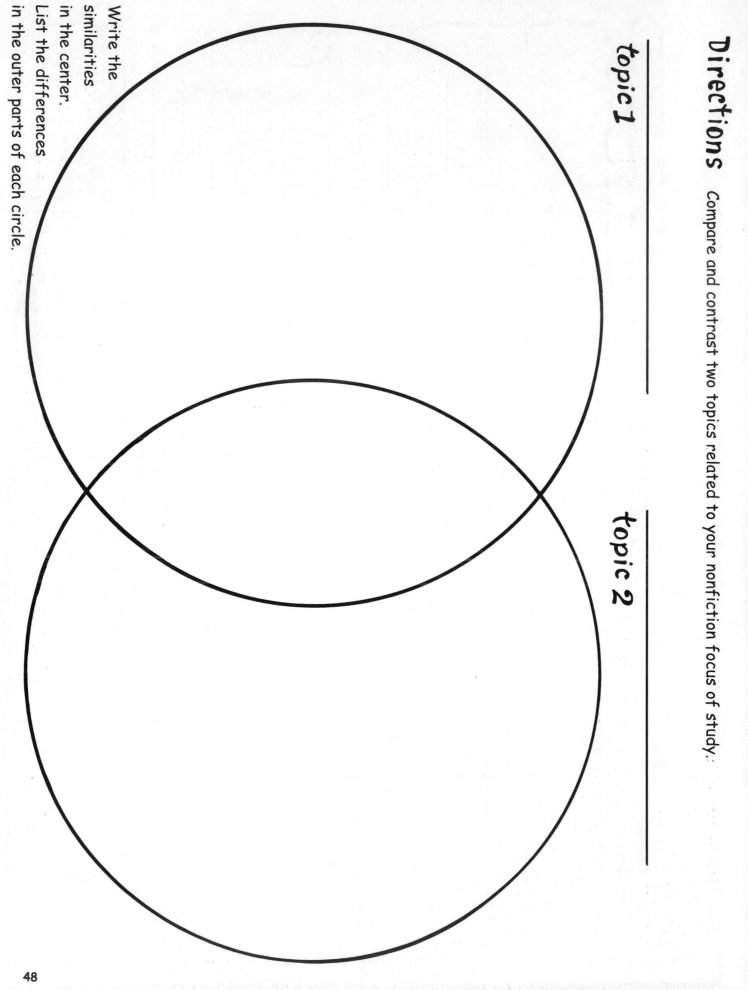

Directions Compare and contrast two topics related to your nonfiction focus of study.

topic 1

topic 2

Write the
similarities
in the center.
List the differences
in the outer parts
of each circle.

Scholastic Teaching Resources • Grades 4–6 Graphic Organizer Booklets • Nonfiction, page 5

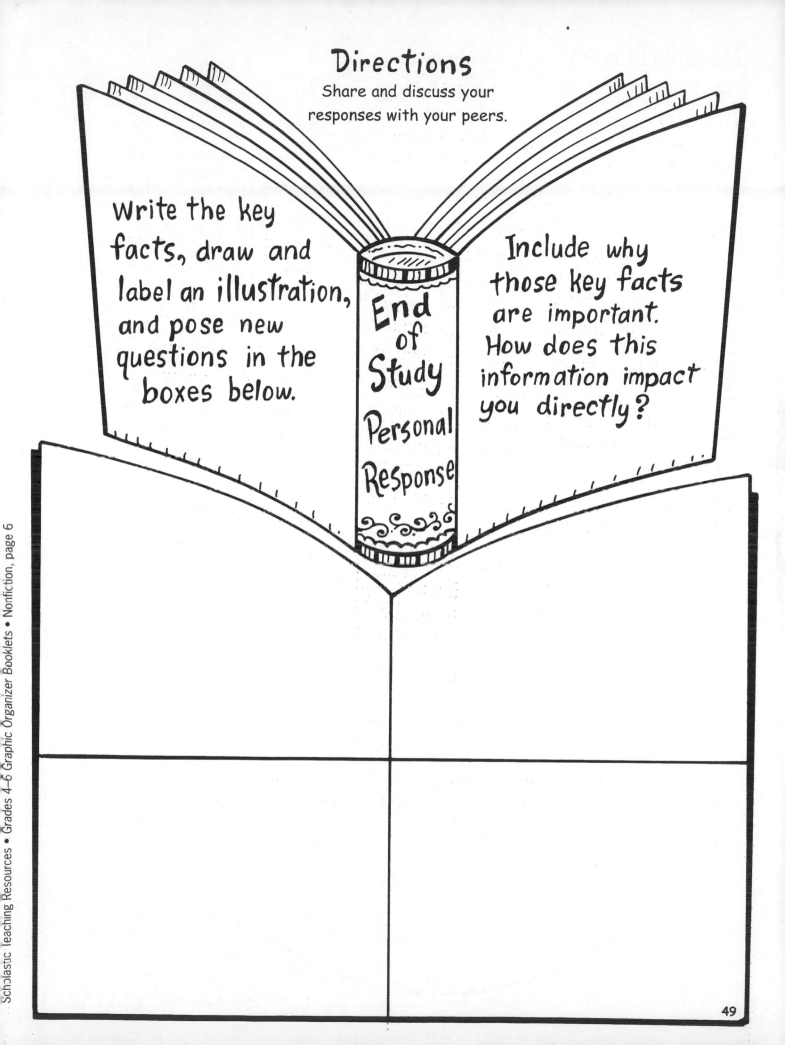

Directions

Share and discuss your responses with your peers.

Write the key facts, draw and label an illustration, and pose new questions in the boxes below.

End of Study Personal Response

Include why those key facts are important. How does this information impact you directly?

Helpful Hints for the Fiction Booklet:

- **Model each activity** as often as necessary so students understand its purpose as well as the directions.

- **Remind students to preview** the pages of the booklet so they are aware of pre-reading, during-reading, and post-reading activities.

- **Theme is a difficult concept** for students to grasp. Model this process by sharing your thoughts aloud as you decide on a theme. The ensuing discussion will help students learn how to use story events to focus on a theme.

- **Many of the activities** in this book can be expanded into writing responses. Think about using these ideas to spark other writing activities.

Exemplary text:

The Butterfly by Patricia Polacco (Philomel Books, 2000)

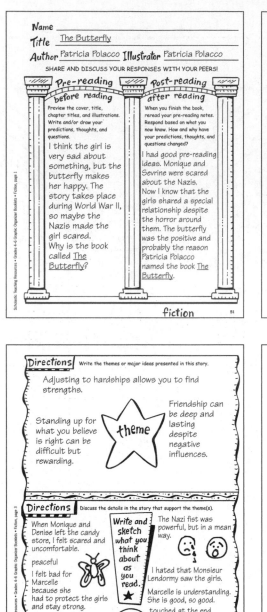

Name _____

Title __The Butterfly__

Author __Patricia Polacco__ Illustrator __Patricia Polacco__

SHARE AND DISCUSS YOUR RESPONSES WITH YOUR PEERS!

Pre-reading *before reading*

Preview the cover, title, chapter titles, and illustrations. Write and/or draw your predictions, thoughts, and questions.

I think the girl is very sad about something, but the butterfly makes her happy. The story takes place during World War II, so maybe the Nazis made the girl scared. Why is the book called The Butterfly?

Post-reading *after reading*

When you finish the book, reread your pre-reading notes. Respond based on what you now know. How and why have your predictions, thoughts, and questions changed?

I had good pre-reading ideas. Monique and Sevrine were scared about the Nazis. Now I know that the girls shared a special relationship despite the horror around them. The butterfly was the positive and probably the reason Patricia Polacco named the book The Butterfly.

fiction   51

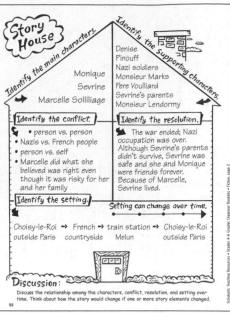

Story House

Identify the main characters.

Monique
Sevrine
Marcelle Solliliage

Identify the supporting characters.

Denise
Pinouff
Nazi soldiers
Monsieur Marks
Pere Voulliard
Sevrine's parents
Monsieur Lendormy

Identify the conflict.
- person vs. person
- Nazis vs. French people
- person vs. self
- Marcelle did what she believed was right even though it was risky for her and her family

Identify the resolution.
The war ended; Nazi occupation was over. Although Sevrine's parents didn't survive, Sevrine was safe and she and Monique were friends forever. Because of Marcelle, Sevrine lived.

Identify the setting.   Setting can change over time.

Choisy-le-Roi outside Paris → French countryside → train station Melun → Choisy-le-Roi outside Paris

Discussion: Discuss the relationship among the characters, conflict, resolution, and setting over time. Think about how the story would change if one or more story elements changed.

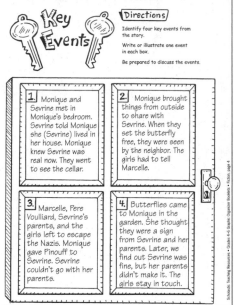

Directions Write the themes or major ideas presented in this story.

Adjusting to hardships allows you to find strengths.

Standing up for what you believe is right can be difficult but rewarding.

theme

Friendship can be deep and lasting despite negative influences.

Directions Discuss the details in the story that support the theme(s).

When Monique and Denise left the candy store, I felt scared and uncomfortable.

peaceful

I felt bad for Marcelle because she had to protect the girls and stay strong. How can they live without knowing what will happen next?

Write and sketch what you think about as you read.

The Nazi fist was powerful, but in a mean way.

I hated that Monsieur Lendormy saw the girls.

Marcelle is understanding. She is good, so good. touched at the end

Story Doodle → separated ←

Key Events

Directions

Identify four key events from the story.

Write or illustrate one event in each box.

Be prepared to discuss the events.

1. Monique and Sevrine met in Monique's bedroom. Sevrine told Monique she (Sevrine) lived in her house. Monique knew Sevrine was real now. They went to see the cellar.

2. Monique brought things from outside to share with Sevrine. When they set the butterfly free, they were seen by the neighbor. The girls had to tell Marcelle.

3. Marcelle, Pere Voulliard, Sevrine's parents, and the girls left to escape the Nazis. Monique gave Pinouff to Sevrine. Sevrine couldn't go with her parents.

4. Butterflies came to Monique in the garden. She thought they were a sign from Sevrine and her parents. Later, we find out Sevrine was fine, but her parents didn't make it. The girls stay in touch.

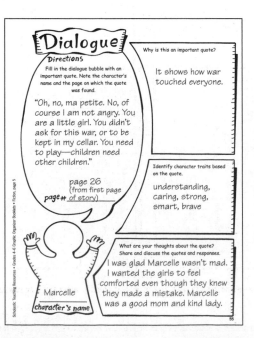

Dialogue

Directions

Fill in the dialogue bubble with an important quote. Note the character's name and the page on which the quote was found.

"Oh, no, ma petite. No, of course I am not angry. You are a little girl. You didn't ask for this war, or to be kept in my cellar. You need to play—children need other children."

page 26 (from first page of story)
page #

Marcelle
character's name

Why is this an important quote?

It shows how war touched everyone.

Identify character traits based on the quote.

understanding, caring, strong, smart, brave

What are your thoughts about the quote? Share and discuss the quotes and responses.

I was glad Marcelle wasn't mad. I wanted the girls to feel comforted even though they knew they made a mistake. Marcelle was a good mom and kind lady.

Put It Together

Directions

Choose 2 characters, events, quotes, settings, or problems from the story. Share how each relates or fits into your life.

1. Marcelle helped Jewish people escape the Nazis. She did what she felt was right.
story

1. When a group of kids was making fun of another kid, I stood up to them to protect him. It was hard at first.
your life

2. Monique and Sevrine were friends, but they had to be apart. They remained close even when they weren't together.
story

2. When I was young, my good friend had to move. Even though we don't see each other often, we're still friends after all these years, just like Sevrine and Monique.
your life

Name _____

Title _____

Author _____ Illustrator _____

SHARE AND DISCUSS YOUR RESPONSES WITH YOUR PEERS!

Pre-reading

before reading

Preview the cover, title, chapter titles, and illustrations. Write and/or draw your predictions, thoughts, and questions.

Post-reading

after reading

When you finish the book, reread your pre-reading notes. Respond based on what you now know. How and why have your predictions, thoughts, and questions changed?

fiction

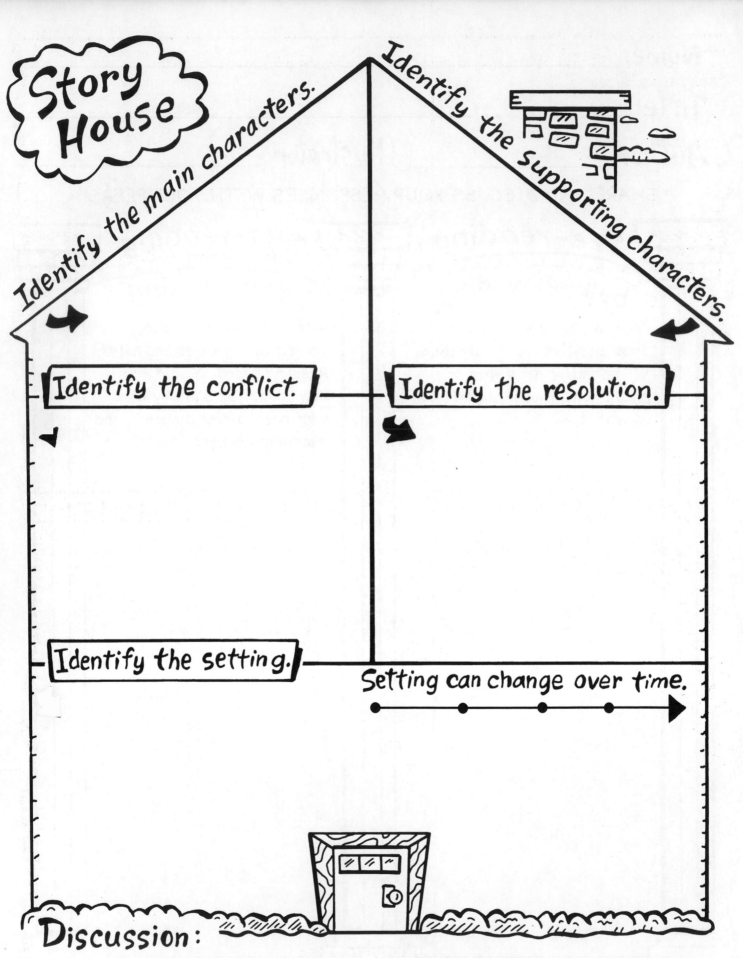

Story House

Identify the main characters.

Identify the supporting characters.

Identify the conflict.

Identify the resolution.

Identify the setting.

Setting can change over time.

Discussion:

Discuss the relationship among the characters, conflict, resolution, and setting over time. Think about how the story would change if one or more story elements changed.

Scholastic Teaching Resources • Grades 4–6 Graphic Organizer Booklets • Fiction, page 2

Directions Write the themes or major ideas presented in this story.

theme

Directions Discuss the details in the story that support the theme(s).

Write and sketch what you think about as you read. ★

Story Doodle

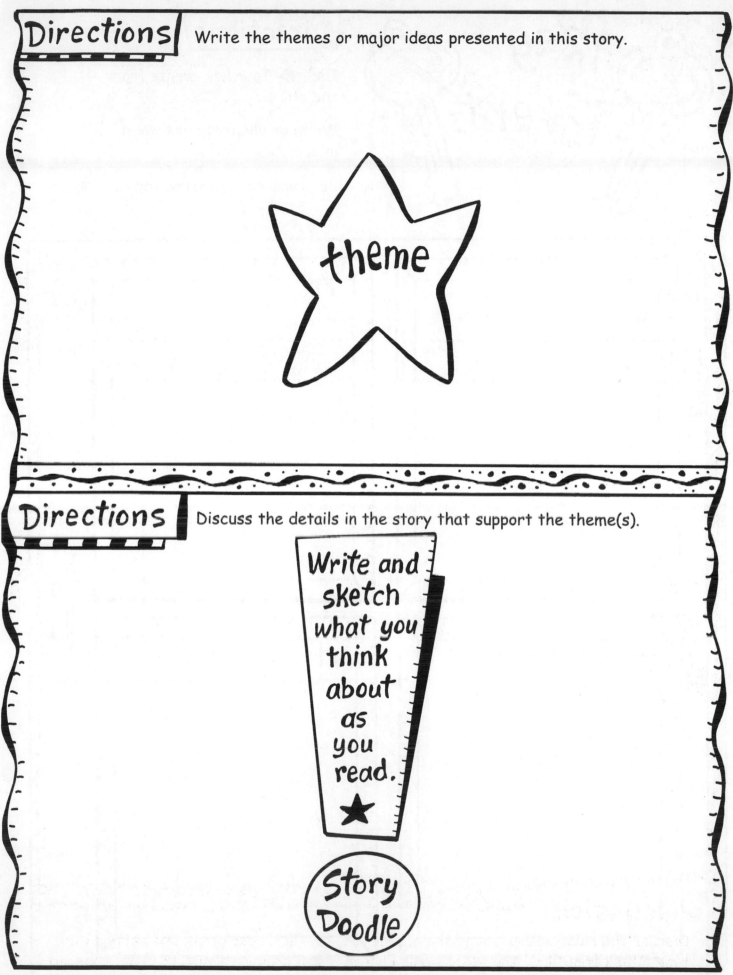

Key Events

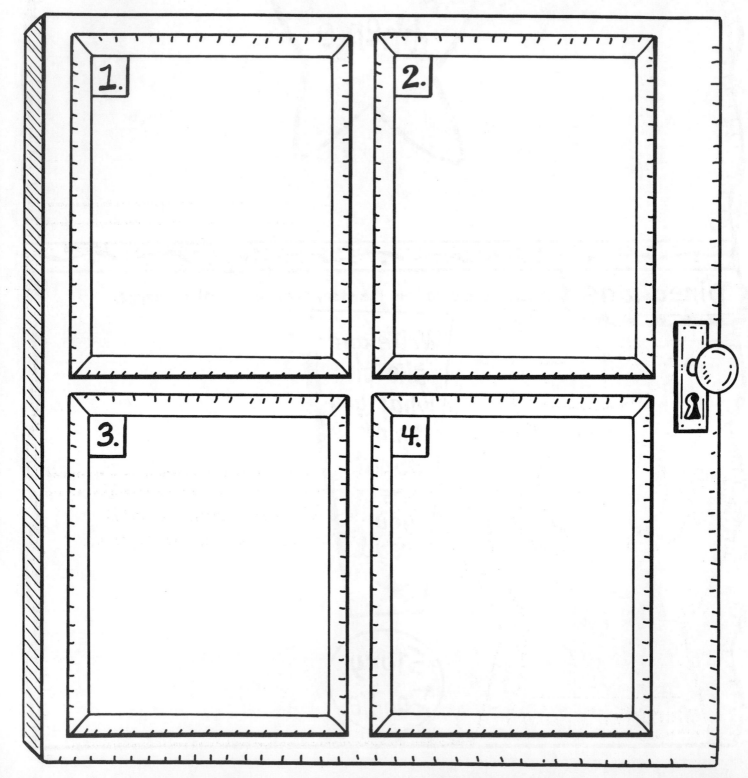

1.

2.

3.

4.

Dialogue

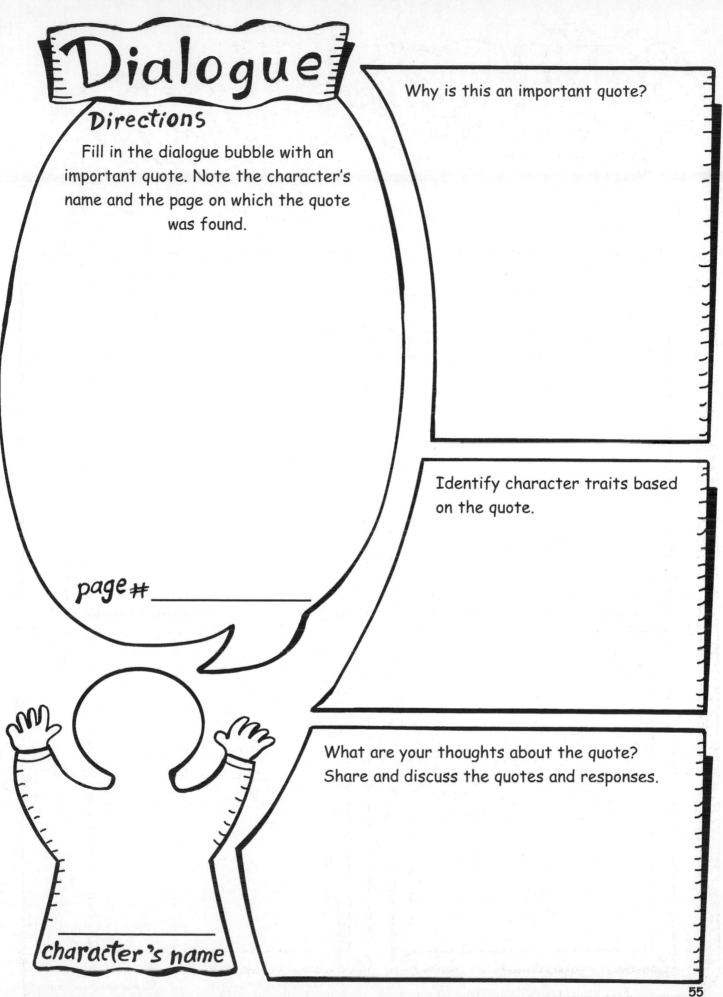

Directions

Fill in the dialogue bubble with an important quote. Note the character's name and the page on which the quote was found.

page # _____

character's name

Why is this an important quote?

Identify character traits based on the quote.

What are your thoughts about the quote? Share and discuss the quotes and responses.

Put It Together

Directions

Choose 2 characters, events, quotes, settings, or problems from the story. Share how each relates or fits into your life.

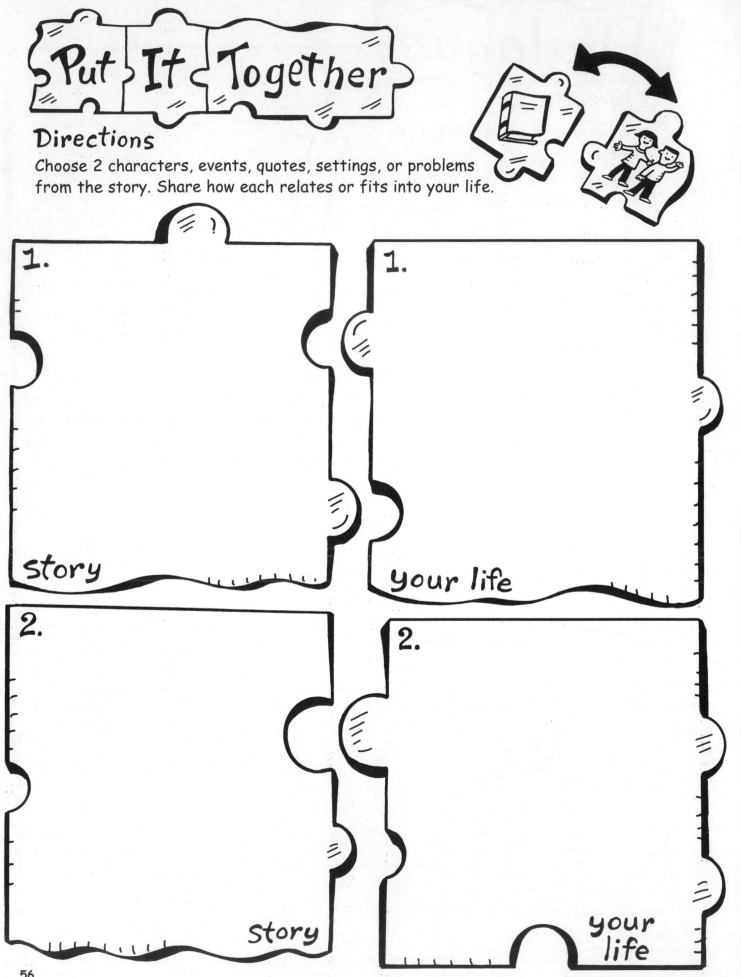

1.

story

1.

your life

2.

story

2.

your life

Scholastic Teaching Resources • Grades 4–6 Graphic Organizer Booklets • Fiction, page 6

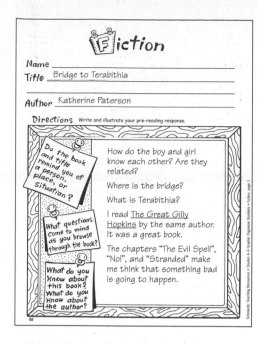

Fiction

Name _____
Title Bridge to Terabithia

Author Katherine Paterson

Directions Write and illustrate your pre-reading response.

Do the book and title remind you of a person, place, or situation?

What questions come to mind as you browse through the book?

What do you know about this book? What do you know about the author?

How do the boy and girl know each other? Are they related?

Where is the bridge?

What is Terabithia?

I read The Great Gilly Hopkins by the same author. It was a great book.

The chapters "The Evil Spell", "No!", and "Stranded" make me think that something bad is going to happen.

58

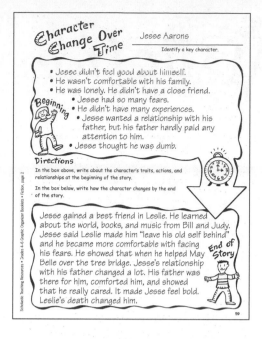

Character Change Over Time

Jesse Aarons
Identify a key character.

Beginning
- Jesse didn't feel good about himself.
- He wasn't comfortable with his family.
- He was lonely. He didn't have a close friend.
- Jesse had so many fears.
- He didn't have many experiences.
- Jesse wanted a relationship with his father, but his father hardly paid any attention to him.
- Jesse thought he was dumb.

Directions
In the box above, write about the character's traits, actions, and relationships at the beginning of the story.

In the box below, write how the character changes by the end of the story.

End of Story
Jesse gained a best friend in Leslie. He learned about the world, books, and music from Bill and Judy. Jesse said Leslie made him "leave his old self behind" and he became more comfortable with facing his fears. He showed that when he helped May Belle over the tree bridge. Jesse's relationship with his father changed a lot. His father was there for him, comforted him, and showed that he really cared. It made Jesse feel bold. Leslie's death changed him.

59

Directions
Read the quotes your teacher has supplied, or quote two critical sections of text from the story. (Note page numbers.)

Be prepared to discuss the significance of each quote.

Quote 1
"She had tricked him. She had made him leave his old self behind and come into her world, and then before he was really at home in it but too late to go back, she had left him stranded there—like an astronaut wandering about on the moon. Alone." p. 114

Quote 2
"Now it was time for him to move out. She wasn't there, so he must go for both of them. It was up to him to pay back to the world in beauty and caring what Leslie had loaned him in vision and strength." p. 126

Directions
During or after reading, list any unknown words in context or note the interesting use of language. (Note page numbers.) For new vocabulary words, brainstorm additional sentences. Think about synonyms, antonyms, and any connotations. Be prepared to share and discuss your choices and thoughts.

obediently: "Shoulders sagged but the boys backed away obediently" p. 24
The children listen obediently in class.
antonym: defiantly
"Momma would be as mad as flies in a fruit jar if they woke her up this time of day." p. 1
"...but he buried his head in the rich sound of the words and he let himself be wrapped warmly around in the feel of the Burke's brilliance." p. 69

60

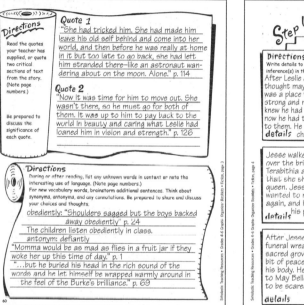

Step Up to Inferencing

Directions
Write details to support your inference(s) in the boxes below. After Leslie died, Jesse thought maybe Terabithia was a place to get strong and move on. He knew he had fears, but now he had to stand up to them. He knew he'd **details** changed.

Jesse walked May Belle over the bridge to Terabithia and hinted that she should be queen. Jesse also wanted to milk Bessie again, and he wanted his paints back. **details**

After Jesse put the funeral wreath in the sacred grove, he felt a bit of peace go through his body. He admitted to May Belle it was OK to be scared. **details**

+ common sense
+ your ideas
+ personal knowledge

Inference(s)

Use information from the story and your personal knowledge to make an inference about a character or situation in the story. The author will not give you this information directly. You must make a reasonable guess or an inference.

Jesse will overcome some of his fears and become a stronger, different person. Leslie helped him grow up fast.

Building a bridge is more than a chapter title or a book title. Jesse built a strong bridge to cross into Terabithia and a personal bridge to cross into new situations, relationships, and experiences.

61

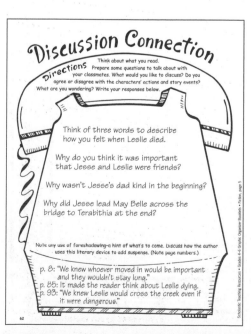

Discussion Connection

Directions Think about what you read. Prepare some questions to talk about with your classmates. What would you like to discuss? Do you agree or disagree with the characters' actions and story events? What are you wondering? Write your responses below.

Think of three words to describe how you felt when Leslie died.

Why do you think it was important that Jesse and Leslie were friends?

Why wasn't Jesse's dad kind in the beginning?

Why did Jesse lead May Belle across the bridge to Terabithia at the end?

Note any use of foreshadowing—a hint of what's to come. Discuss how the author uses this literary device to add suspense. (Note page numbers.)

p. 8: "We knew whoever moved in would be important and they wouldn't stay long."
p. 85: It made the reader think about Leslie dying.
p. 93: "We knew Leslie would cross the creek even if it were dangerous."

62

Personal Response

Directions
During or after reading, record your personal thoughts and questions under each heading.

Heading		Personal Response
?	question	Why didn't Jesse want to be friends with Leslie at first?
!	was surprised about	I was surprised when Leslie died.
♡	liked	I liked when Jesse and Leslie spent time together at Terabithia.
	didn't like	I didn't like it when Leslie died. I didn't like it when Jesse's parents were mean to him.
⟳	would change	I would want Leslie to live so she and Jesse could be friends.
	made me think about...	Leslie's death made me think about how special my friends are.
	didn't understand	I didn't understand why Leslie's parents didn't have a TV even though they could afford one.

63

Helpful Hints for the Fiction Booklet:

- Model each activity as often as necessary so students understand its purpose as well as the directions.

- Remind students to preview the pages of the booklet so they are aware of pre-reading, during-reading, and post-reading activities.

- When students think about a character, remind them to study actions, words, and thoughts to determine the character's traits. By focusing on specific quotes, students will begin to grasp how to better understand the character and his or her role in the story.

- For page 3, you may want to supply two quotes for the students to respond to. Write the quotes on the page before duplicating and distributing it.

- When focusing on new vocabulary, give students multiple exposure to the words beyond the story context. Encourage them to think about synonyms and antonyms, multiple meanings, and connotations. To determine whether students have mastered the word and not just memorized it, ask them to use the word in a sentence.

Exemplary text:

Bridge to Terabithia by Katherine Paterson (HarperCollins, 1977).

iction

Name _____

Title _____

_____

Author _____

Directions Write and illustrate your pre-reading response.

Do the book and title remind you of a person, place, or situation?

What questions come to mind as you browse through the book?

What do you know about this book? What do you know about the author?

Scholastic Teaching Resources • Grades 4–6 Graphic Organizer Booklets • Fiction, page 1

Character Change Over Time

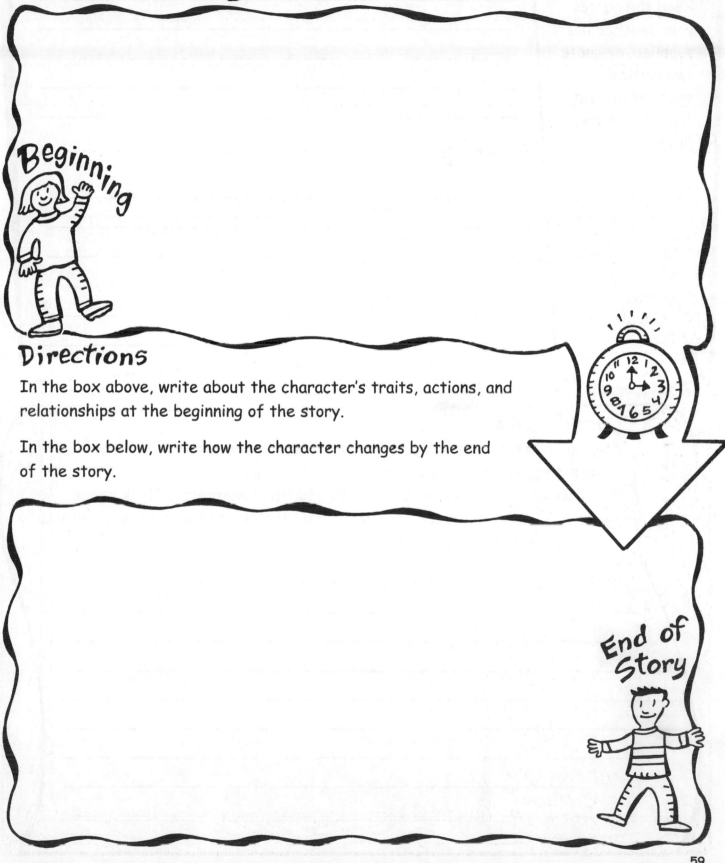

Beginning

Directions

In the box above, write about the character's traits, actions, and relationships at the beginning of the story.

In the box below, write how the character changes by the end of the story.

End of Story

Read the quotes your teacher has supplied, or quote two critical sections of text from the story. (Note page numbers.)

Be prepared to discuss the significance of each quote.

Quote 1

_____
_____
_____
_____
_____
_____

Quote 2

_____
_____
_____
_____
_____
_____
_____

Directions

During or after reading, list any unknown words in context or note the interesting use of language. (Note page numbers.)

For new vocabulary words, brainstorm additional sentences. Think about synonyms, antonyms, and any connotations. Be prepared to share and discuss your choices and thoughts.

_____
_____
_____
_____
_____
_____
_____
_____

Step Up to Inferencing

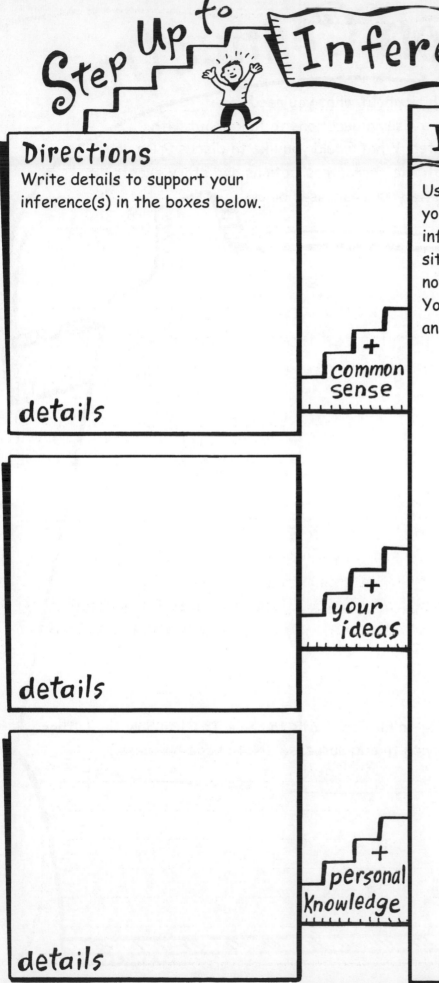

Directions

Write details to support your inference(s) in the boxes below.

details

details

details

+ common sense

+ your ideas

+ personal knowledge

Inference (s)

Use information from the story and your personal knowledge to make an inference about a character or situation in the story. The author will not give you this information directly. You must make a reasonable guess or an inference.

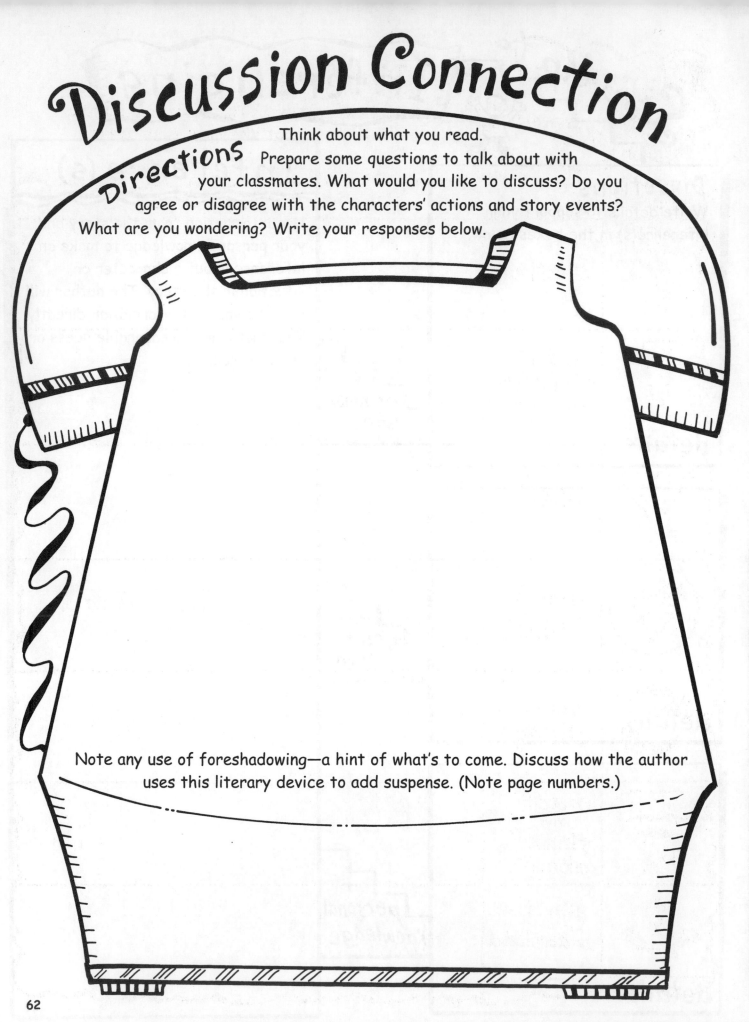

Discussion Connection

Directions Think about what you read. Prepare some questions to talk about with your classmates. What would you like to discuss? Do you agree or disagree with the characters' actions and story events? What are you wondering? Write your responses below.

Note any use of foreshadowing—a hint of what's to come. Discuss how the author uses this literary device to add suspense. (Note page numbers.)

Scholastic Teaching Resources • Grades 4–6 Graphic Organizer Booklets • Fiction, page 5

Directions

During or after reading, record your personal thoughts and questions under each heading.

Heading		Personal Response
?	question	
!	was surprised about	
♥	liked	
(crossed-out ♥)	didn't like	
(cycle arrows)	would change	
(person thinking)	made me think about...	
(person with ?)	didn't understand	

Notes